GEO

10 Things You Need to Know About

Throwing Parties

by Jen Jones

Capstone press®

Mankato, Minnesota

Snap Books are published by Capstone Press,
151 Good Counsel Drive, P.O. Box 669, Mankato, Minnesota 56002.
www.capstonepress.com

Library of Congress Cataloging-in-Publication Data
Jones, Jen.
Throwing parties / by Jen Jones.
p. cm. —(Snap books. 10 things you need to know about)
Summary: "Provides instructions and helpful hints for planning and hosting parties,
including tips on invitations, food, music, and games"—Provided by publisher.
Includes bibliographical references and index.
ISBN-13: 978-1-4296-0130-6 (hardcover)
ISBN-10: 1-4296-0130-2 (hardcover)
1. Children's parties—Juvenile literature. 2. Parties—Juvenile literature. I. Title. II. Series.
GV1205.J65 2008
793.2'1—dc22   2007001309

Editors: Wendy Dieker and Christine Peterson
Designer: Juliette Peters
Photo Researchers: Charlene Deyle and Jo Miller
Photo Stylist: Kelly Garvin

Photo Credits:
Capstone Press/Karon Dubke, 6, 7, 11, 12–13 (middle), 16–17, 17 (right), 18–19 (all), 24–25; Corbis/Tom Stewart, 21;
Corbis/zefa/Alexander Scott, 22; Getty Images Inc./The Image Bank/M. Nader, cover; Getty Images Inc./Taxi/Tony
Anderson, 5; Index Stock Imagery/Bob Winsett, 8–9; Michele Torma Lee, 32; Shutterstock, 13; Shutterstock/Alex James
Bramwell, 23 (left all), 25, 30; Shutterstock/Andrey Popov, 24; Shutterstock/Carlos Arranz, 27; Shutterstock/Danny
E. Hooks, 4; Shutterstock/Ingvald Kaldhussater, 26; Shutterstock/Iryna Kurthan, 12; Shutterstock/James Steidl, back
cover; Shutterstock/Jo Ann Snover, 20; Shutterstock/Melanie Taylor, 23 (bottom right) Shutterstock/Stephen Coburn, 9;
Shutterstock/Vincent Giordano, 10 (all), 31; SuperStock Inc./ Stock Image, 15

1 2 3 4 5 6 12 11 10 09 08 07

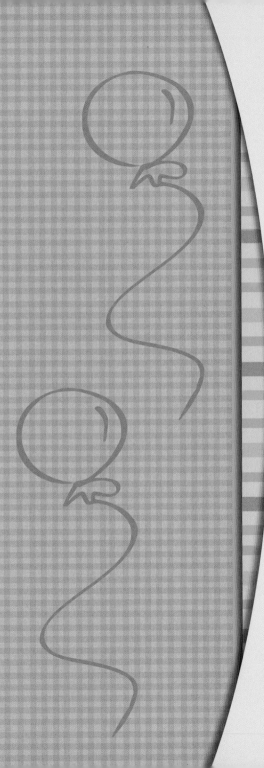

Table of Contents

Introduction

Backyard barbecues and glitzy birthday bashes. Crazy costume parties and silly girls-only sleepovers. Game nights and get-down dance marathons. As a hostess, you're in the driver's seat of designing your special event. The party possibilities are endless.

Hosting a party can be tons of fun, but it involves lots of work. Many preparations must take place in the weeks before the event. This book will help you plan your party from start to finish. From the perfect outfit to the tastiest party food, we'll give you all the ingredients for the ultimate event.

Throw a million-dollar party on a dime

Ever watched MTV's *My Super Sweet 16*? No party on this show is complete without celeb music performances and all the fancy trimmings. Those swanky events are enough to make even Rachael Ray green with envy.

Yet not everyone can spend like they have a bottomless bank account. Luckily, it's possible to roll out the red carpet for your guests without breaking the bank. Here are a few ideas on how to throw a bash on a budget:

- Create homemade invitations.
- Serve easy and cheap finger foods.
- Make the party a potluck where guests bring food to share.
- Make a killer party mix on your player rather than hiring a DJ.

Saving on costs doesn't mean scrimping on fun. In the end, it's about having a great time.

2 Invite guests in style

In today's high-tech world, there are endless ways to get the word out. You could send a mass text message or e-mail a cute Evite of your own design. Some people even go the old-school route and mail invitations. Or you could invite guests in person.

Certain kinds of parties call for creative invitations. For instance, a going away party might have invitations in the style of a plane ticket. A movie outing could have invites that look like a director's slate or a movie poster. Computer programs like Photoshop and Microsoft Word make these ideas easy to put in motion. Use your imagination!

Trusty Tip

Don't forget to ask guests to RSVP. You'll need to know how many people are coming in order to get enough food and drinks. RSVPs can be given by phone, e-mail, or in person—whatever works for you.

Happy Birthday

For : Christine   Time : 5:30

Date : July 12

Place : 232 Sunshine Place

Mankato

R.S.V.P. :   Julie 555-2341

3 Put your head together with your parents

We'd all love to be the person in charge, but until age 18, that's just not an option. It's important to have parents or guardians at your party. They can make sure everyone is safe and that things don't spiral out of control. You don't want your friends ruining your home or your stuff. Having parents there keeps everyone in check.

Before the party, meet with your parents. Talk to them about how much they are willing to let you spend. They should also get a say in where the party is held, how many people can come, and how long the party will last. You can also work together to make a shopping list for food, drinks, and supplies. Cooperation is key for a killer event.

4 Jazz up the joint with themes and party favors!

Any type of party is fun, but theme parties take fun to a whole new level. Examples of themes might include murder mysteries, retro dress-up parties, or Hawaiian luaus. At a theme party, invite guests to come dressed in costumes. But the fun doesn't stop with the outfits. Colorful decorations and special games to go with your theme will really get the party started.

Party favors can also make a lasting impression. These small gifts record the hostess' name, the date, and the occasion. Favors can be small, like a chocolate kiss for a Valentine's Day party. They can also be personal, like a picture frame or a mix CD. With party favors, guests leave with a lasting memory of your party.

Party Mix

Dream Themes

Set yourself apart with these out-of-the-ordinary ideas:

❀ **Wig Out:** Everyone wears wigs.
❀ **Fun-Due:** Everyone samples different fondues.
❀ **Scaryoke:** Everyone sings karaoke in monster costumes.

5 Party like the adult you're not

Parties are a great excuse to play grown-up—if only for a night. Adults get to stay up late and dine on fancy food and drinks. Guess what? You can too! Discover your inner party diva and impress your friends with these beyond yummy recipes.

BERRY GOOD LEMONADE

This lemonade is full of surprises. Combine one can of juice concentrate (your choice: strawberry, raspberry, or cranberry) with one can of water. Pour the mixture into two ice cube trays and freeze. Once the "berry good" ice cubes are good to go, serve them in yummy lemonade. As the cubes melt in the drink, it tastes better and better. Add sugar around the rim of the glass for some extra sassy sweetness.

SPICE OF LIFE SALSA DIP

Turn up the heat with this easy-to-make salsa mix. In a medium serving bowl, stir together one jar of salsa and 1 cup (240 mL) of sour cream. Add 2 tablespoons (30 mL) of chopped fresh cilantro. Serve with tortilla chips, and dip to your heart's content.

6 Decorations can set the perfect mood

The right decorations can give a total makeover to the most boring basements or backyards. While balloons or streamers might seem like kid stuff, there are tons of other ways to jazz up the joint.

Use simple touches to make the party area an elegant mealtime place. Patterned tablecloths or fun centerpieces can set a festive mood. Some inexpensive centerpiece ideas are goldfish bowls, floating candles, or fancy bowls filled with potpourri.

Lighting plays a big part in changing up the look. Hang colorful store-bought paper lanterns around the party area. Or make an outdoor walkway out of luminary bags. To make this festive party light, just place a scoop of sand and a tea light inside a small paper bag.

Place Cards

If you are planning a sit-down meal, fun and fancy place cards can tell guests where they should sit. Use place cards as a way for guests to meet. Dress up your place cards with decorations to add a little sparkle to your party table.

7 Don't wait until the last minute

No matter how soon you start planning, parties tend to sneak up on you. A stressed hostess is no fun. So how can you avoid rushing around with last-minute errands? Like a good Girl Scout, it's a must to be prepared. Follow this time line for smooth party sailing:

One Month Ahead
* Pick a date.
* Talk with your parents about the details.
* Choose a place, and reserve if necessary.
* Make the guest list.

Two or Three Weeks Ahead
* Send the invites.
* Shop for decorations and party favors.
* Figure out the food and drink offerings.
* Plan and buy materials for any games.

Week of Party
* Shop for and/or order food and drinks.
* Buy party supplies.
* Contact guests who haven't responded.
* Clean.

Day of Party
* Decorate and set up.
* Have a blast!

8 Tops on the to-do list: what to wear!

To dress for party success, a hostess needs to set herself apart from the pack. Since it's your special day, you might want to consider splurging on a new outfit. There's no better time than your own party to step out in style!

Some adventurous party girls love to dress outside their everyday wardrobes. If you're feeling daring, go glam with a feather boa or sparkly shades. If you are throwing a theme party, dress the part. Who knows? Your fun duds could start a new style trend!

9 Be a "hostess with the mostest"

At a party, guests look to the hostess to set the social tone. Your attitude can be catching, so make sure it's a good one. A smile and friendly greeting go a long way. At some parties, not all of the guests will know each other. It's your job to introduce people and "get the party started."

If you come across an awkward conversation, help your guests find something in common. Odds are they might enjoy the same sports or TV shows. No one knows your guests better than you do, so use that knowledge to connect them. Telling a funny story or joke is also a great icebreaker.

10 When in doubt, "game on!"

Fun activities and games are a great way to keep guests entertained. Get a head start by checking out our mini-guide to the wide world of games and activities:

• Icebreaker games help guests learn each other's names and interests. When inviting different groups of friends, it's a plus to plan these types of games while the guests are arriving or toward the beginning of the party.

• Board games can liven up the party and get guests to mingle. Choose games that require lots of teamwork. Playing Catch Phrase, Scene It, or Pictionary can really liven up a room.

• Outdoor games like water balloon tosses or three-legged races can also be a laugh riot. While games like this often require extra supplies, the extra money might be worth it to see your guests laughing.

Got Game?

Dare to be different with Truth or Dare Jenga. This game brings together two party favorites. Players take turns choosing between "truth or dare." To play, use a marker to write safe and appropriate dares on all of the Jenga pieces. If a player chooses "dare," he or she must take a piece out of the Jenga tower. After completing the dare, they get to choose someone else to go. The game continues until the tower topples.

A Few More Things You Need to Know

Dance to the beat of your own drum

Get your guests on their feet with a killer music mix. At the start, make sure not to crank up the music too loud. Guests will want to hear each other talk. As time passes, pump up the volume with upbeat tunes everyone knows by heart.

Be prepared to deal with problems

No party is perfect, and something is bound to go wrong. Whether it's a fly in the punch or a fight between friends, try to stay calm. It's all about fun, not being frazzled.

Tell your guests to "Say cheese!"

If you don't capture your party on camera, it's almost like it never happened. Besides taking your own pics, you can also pass out disposable cameras and let your guests go to town. Picture perfect!

Embrace the element of surprise

Advertising a "surprise" is sure to get guests curious enough to come. Surprises could range from a visit from an old friend to a local DJ everyone loves.

Thank-you notes are a class act

Thank-you notes are the perfect way to thank guests for presents—or simply for their presence. Set out a guestbook at the party to collect addresses. Sending small notes or a digital photo of the party shows class and is the mark of a good hostess.

A party to remember!

Remember, party day is the time to relax and enjoy your event. Weeks of party prep are about to pay off. Just add fun and you've got a recipe for a party to remember!

Quiz

Which Party Girl Are You?

Hardly anyone you've invited has shown up yet. What do you do?
A Chill out. Less is more!
B Enjoy the company of those who are present.
C Immediately send out a mass text to all your BFFs.

What's your favorite dance song?
A "We are Family" by Sister Sledge
B "Get the Party Started" by Pink
C "In Da Club" by 50 Cent

Where are you most likely to be spotted on a Saturday night?
A Dinner and a flick with a few close friends
B Singing your heart out at karaoke
C Dancing in the city at the hottest under-18 club

Which cable network do you love to watch?
A Disney Channel
B The N
C Style Network

You get a free swag bag at a big Hollywood party. What item in the bag are you most excited about?
A Free one-year subscription to Netflix
B A swank handbag
C T-Mobile Sidekick so you can stay in better touch with all your friends

Which theme party best suits your personality?
A Murder Mystery
B '80s Prom
C Hawaiian Luau

Your best friends throw you a surprise party. How do you react?
A You're a bit embarrassed at all the attention, but honored at the same time.
B You're thrilled to see all your friends and family in one place. You don't know whom to hug first!
C You're not surprised at all. Of course all your admirers wanted to do something nice for you.

Which Hollywood heartthrob do you love the most?
A Low-key, smooth singer Justin Timberlake
B Funny guy Nick Cannon
C Party boy Wilmer Valderrama

Which party foul are you most likely to be guilty of?
A Leaving too early
B Telling a horrible joke that makes everyone groan
C Getting into a catfight with another girl

Pick your party motto:
A "Surround me with just a few friends and I'm a happy girl."
B "Life is one big party."
C "Party all night, every night!"

It's the weekend. What are you most looking forward to?
A Relaxing by the pool with a good book
B Shopping with friends
C Going out on the town

What would your most fitting IM name be?
A SweetThing16
B SillyGirlSmilin
C DarlinDiva22

At which party location are you most likely to be found?
A On the couch chatting it up
B Cracking jokes and stealing the mike
C On the dance floor

How many parties do you attend per month?
A Not too many—I like to be more low-key.
B As many as I can—it's all about fun!
C There are so many—who can keep track?

What's your favorite kind of party?
A Sleepover with the girls
B Coed pool party
C Dance marathon

When scoring your answers, A equals 5 points, B equals 3 points, and C equals 1 point. Total them up and find out where you fit into the party girl equation!

1-25 = You love to be the center of attention. You don't just attend the party; you are the party!

26-50 = People flock to your friendly, fun personality at parties. Being a social butterfly comes naturally to you.

51-75 = Spending quality time with friends and family is your fave thing to do. You prefer time with your peeps over being in the spotlight.

29

Glossary

centerpiece (SEN-tur-peese)—a decorative object at the center of a table

luminary (LOO-min-air-ee)—a decorative light; a luminary can be made from a small paper bag filled with sand and a tea light.

occasion (oh-KAY-zshun)—an event or day with a special purpose

potpourri (poh-puh-REE)—a mixture of flowers, herbs, and spices that gives off a pleasant scent

RSVP (AR-ESS-VEE-PEE)—a response as to whether someone can attend a party; RSVP is short for the French words that mean "please respond."

theme (THEEM)—a central idea for a party or event that is reflected in the decoration, food, and dress

Read More

Brian, Sarah Jane. *Party Secrets: Who to Invite, Must-Dance Music, Most-Loved Munchies & Foolproof Fun!* Middleton, Wis.: American Girl, 2003.

Bull, Jane. *The Party Book.* Jane Bull's Things to Make and Do. New York: DK, 2005.

White, Kelly (editor). *The Girls' Life Guide to Great Parties.* New York: Scholastic, 2003.

Internet Sites

FactHound offers a safe, fun way to find Internet sites related to this book. All of the sites on FactHound have been researched by our staff.

Here's how:
1. Visit *www.facthound.com*
2. Choose your grade level.
3. Type in this book ID **1429601302** for age-appropriate sites. You may also browse subjects by clicking on letters, or by clicking on pictures and words.
4. Click on the **Fetch It** button.

FactHound will fetch the best sites for you!

About the Author

A former professional event planner, Jen Jones is a true party girl at heart. When she's not gathering friends for frolic, she makes her living as a freelance writer in Los Angeles. Her stories have been published in magazines such as *American Cheerleader*, *Dance Spirit*, *Ohio Today*, and *Pilates Style*. She has also written for E! Online and PBS Kids. Jones has been a Web site producer for major talk shows such as *The Jenny Jones Show*, *The Sharon Osbourne Show*, and *The Larry Elder Show*. She recently completed several books on gymnastics and fashion for girls.

Index